'10 : I further
in academic crime
or whatever ....
Love,
Emily
4-13-15

SAN FRANCISCO POEMS

City Lights Bookstore
San Francisco

SAN FRANCISCO POEMS
Lawrence Ferlinghetti

POET LAUREATE SERIES NUMBER ①

CITY LIGHTS FOUNDATION
San Francisco

Cover photograph: Massimo Sestini
Cover design & typography: Yolanda Montijo

Library of Congress Cataloging-in-Publication Data

Ferlinghetti, Lawrence.
  San Francisco poems / Lawrence Ferlinghetti.
    p.cm. -- (Poet laureate series ; no. 1)
    ISBN 1-931404-01-1 / 978-1-931404-01-3
    1. San Francisco (Calif.)--Poetry. I. Title. II. Poet laureate series (City Lights
    Foundation) ; no.1.

PS3511.E557 S36 2002
81I'.54--dc21   2001058164

CITY LIGHTS FOUNDATION publications are edited by Lawrence Ferlinghetti
and Nancy J. Peters and published at the City Lights Bookstore, 261 Columbus
Avenue, San Francisco CA 94133.
www.citylights.com

ACKNOWLEDGMENTS

City Lights Foundation gratefully acknowledges New Directions Publishing and City Lights Books for permission to reprint these poems in Lawrence Ferlinghetti's *SAN FRANCISCO POEMS*.

A North Beach Scene
from *Pictures of the Gone World,* City Lights Books, 1955
They Were Putting Up the Statue
from *A Coney Island of the Mind,* New Directions, 1958
Dog
from *A Coney Island of the Mind,* New Directions, 1958
Baseball Canto
from *Open Eye, Open Heart,* New Directions 1973
The Old Italians Dying
from *Landscapes of Living & Dying,* New Directions, 1979
The Great Chinese Dragon
from *Starting from San Francisco,* New Directions, 1958
Great American Waterfront Poem
from *Who Are We Now?* New Directions, 1976
Two Scavengers in a Truck, Two Beautiful People in a Mercedes
from *Landscapes of Living & Dying,* New Directions, 1979
A Report on a Happening in Washington Square, San Francisco
from *These Are My Rivers,* New Directions, 1993
The Artist
from *A Far Rockaway of the Heart,* New Directions, 1997
The Green Street Mortuary Marching Band
from *A Far Rockaway of the Heart,* New Directions, 1997
Bouncer's Bar
from *A Far Rockaway of the Heart,* New Directions, 1997
I Saw One of Them
from *A Far Rockaway of the Heart,* New Directions, 1997
At the Golden Gate
from *A Far Rockaway of the Heart,* New Directions, 1997
Changing Light
from *How to Paint Sunlight,* New Directions, 2001
Yachts in the Sun
from *How to Paint Sunlight,* New Directions, 2001

TABLE OF CONTENTS

© Gardner Haskell, 1995

INAUGURAL ADDRESS

I certainly was surprised to be named Poet Laureate of this far-out city on the left side of the world, and I gratefully accept, for as I told the Mayor, "How could I refuse?" I'd rather be Poet Laureate of San Francisco than anywhere because this city has always been a poetic center, a frontier for free poetic life, with perhaps more poets and more poetry readers than any city in the world.

But we are in danger of losing it. In fact, we are in danger of losing much more than that. All that made this City so unique in the first place seems to be going down the tube at an alarming rate.

This week's *Bay Guardian* has the results of a survey that "reveals a city undergoing a radical transformation — from a diverse metropolis that welcomed immigrants and refugees from around the world to a homogeneous, wealthy enclave."

The gap between the rich and the poor in San Francisco increased more than forty percent in just two years recently. "San Francisco may soon become the first fully gentrified city in America, the urban equivalent of a gated bedroom community," says Daniel Zoll in the *Guardian*. "Now it's becoming almost impossible for a lot of the people who have made this such a world-class city — people who have been the heart and soul of the city for decades — from the fishers and pasta makers and blue-collar workers to the jazz musicians to the beat poets to the hippies to the punks and so many others — to exist here anymore. And when you've lost that part of the city, you've lost San Francisco."

And Richard Walker, head of geography at UC Berkeley has said, "It means a one-dimensional city, a more conservative city — one that will no longer be a fount of social innovation and rebellion from below. Just another American city, a corporate city — a fate it has resisted for generations."

When I arrived in the City in 1950, I came overland by train and took ferry from the Oakland mole to the Ferry Building. And San Francisco looked like some Mediterranean port — a small white city, with mostly white buildings — a little like Tunis seen from seaward. I thought perhaps it was Atlantis, risen from the sea. I certainly saw North Beach especially as a poetic place, as poetic as some quartiers in Paris, as any place in old Europa, as poetic as any place great poets and painters had found inspiration. And this was the first poem I wrote here . . . a North Beach scene:

Away above a harborful
                                of caulkless houses
    among the charley noble chimneypots
                        of a rooftop rigged with clotheslines
            a woman pastes up sails
                                upon the wind
    hanging out her morning sheets
                                        with wooden pins
                        O lovely mammal
                                            her nearly naked breasts
                    throw taut shadows
                                    as she stretches up
to hang at last the last of her
                            so white washed sins
        but it is wetly amorous
                            and winds itself about her
            clinging to her skin
                            So caught with arms

                                  upraised

      she tosses back her head

                   in voiceless laughter

   and in choiceless gesture then

                       shakes out gold hair

while in the reachless seascape spaces

           between the blown white shrouds

  stand out the bright steamers

                      to kingdom come

But this past weekend North Beach looked like a theme-park, literally overrun by tourists, and kitsch was king.

What happened to it? What makes for a free poetic life? What destroys the poetry of a city?

Automobiles destroy it, and they destroy more than the poetry. All over America, all over Europe in fact, cities and towns are under assault by the automobile, are being literally destroyed by car culture. But cities are gradually learning that they don't have to let it happen to them. Witness our beautiful new Embarcadero! And in San Francisco right now we have another chance to stop Autogeddon from happening here. Just a few blocks from here, the ugly Central Freeway can be brought down for good if you vote for Proposition E on the November ballot.

And for another destroyer of poetry and peace, how about those killing machines, the Navy's Blue Angels, who have just carried out their annual attack on the City? But the poetic life requires Peace not War. The poetic life of the City, our subjective life, the subjective life of the individual is constantly under attack by all the forces of materialist civilization, by all the forces of our military-industrial perplex, and we don't need these warplanes designed to kill and ludicrously misnamed the Blue Angels. They dive upon our city every year, in a frightening militarist and nationalist display of pure male testosterone. I've seen old Vietnam ladies in Washington Square diving under the benches! Do we really need to be reminded yearly how our planes have bombed Third World countries back to the Stone Age? In San Francisco, of all places, do we really need "bombs bursting in air to prove that our flag is still there"? What would Saint

Francis say? Perhaps the City could disinvite them next year.

I could go on until I'm singing to your snores, but I'll mention just one more destroyer: chain stores, or chain gangs. Corporate chain stores wipe out long-established independents, killing off local color, local traditions, and — in the case of bookstores — literary history. I've been to other great cities on poetry tours and found not a single independent bookstore left in neighborhoods where chain gangs have moved in. It's an old story by now, but it's time to revise a lot of old stories! If so much of this City's population doesn't want chain stores, as the *Bay Guardian* suggests, why can't the City government take a united stand against them?

But to get to the positive side of things, I have quite a wish list for the City. I've proposed that North Beach, with its long literary history including Mark Twain, Jack London, Ina Coolbrith, William Saroyan, and many others including Beat writers, be officially protected as a "historic district," in the manner of the French Quarter in New Orleans, and thus shielded from commercial destruction such as was suffered by the classic old Montgomery Block building, the most famous literary and artistic structure in the West until it was replaced by the Transamerica Pyramid. I do hope someone will pick up this ball and run with it.

And I've already proposed that a small wooden house on Treasure Island or in the Presidio be made a Poet's Cottage where future laureates might live or work and conduct poetry events or even an annual city poetry festival. The Mayor and the important journal *Poetry Flash* are already behind it, so I hope it will happen.

And since we are in the Main Library, let's remember that the center of literate culture in cities has always centered in the great libraries as well as in the great independent bookstores. This Library should have ten million dollars a year to spend on books, more than twice as much as presently allotted. It also needs more space, since evidently this new state-of-the-computer postmodern masterpiece doesn't have as much shelf space as the Old Library next door — that classical Carnegie-style library with its great turn-of-the-century murals — and I believe the people made a great mistake in passing the proposition to remove the building from the library system. It might not be too late to reclaim it as a Library Annex, even though the proposition to get rid of it has already been partially implemented. All it would take is another proposition on the ballot to retrieve it, just as the

Central Freeway proposition may soon very well succeed in reversing an earlier misguided vote.

Other outrageous things on my wish list include: One — give bicycles and pedestrians absolute priority over automobiles, and close much of the original inner city to cars, including Upper Grant Avenue. Two — make the City a center for low-power alternative radio and TV, with tax breaks for the broadcasters. Three — uncover our city's creeks and rivers again and open up the riparian corridors to the Bay. Five — Paint the Golden Gate Bridge golden. Six — tilt Coit Tower — think what it did for Pisa!

And speaking of the literary culture of the city, I'd like to announce that City Lights is just now attempting to create a non-profit foundation so that City Lights may continue through the next century as a literary center and poetic presence in the City. For such a foundation, we need help. Philanthropic literary angels are invited to descend upon us!

II.

Poets, come out of your closets,
Open your windows, open your doors,
You have been holed – up too long
in your closed worlds
. . . .
No time now for the artist to hide
above, beyond, behind the scenes,
indifferent, paring his fingernails,
refining himself out of existence.
No time now for our little literary games,
for our paranoias and hypochondrias,
no time now for fear & loathing,
time now only for light & love.
We have seen the best minds of our generation
destroyed by boredom at poetry readings
. . . .

What I had in mind in the l970s in this "Populist Manifesto"
was for poets to stop mumbling in their beards to private
audiences and say something important to the world. A few

years ago I gave a talk in Michael McClure's class at the California College of Arts & Crafts, the title of which was "Why don't you paint something important?" (There was a graffito on the wall that said "You're so minimal.") Anyway, it was an attempt to pry the artists, like the poets, out of the their hermetic worlds.

Parenthetically, I must say that my manifesto called forth such a cacophony of bad poetry that some editors felt like chanting, "Poets, go back in your closets!"

The manifesto was a not very original Whitmanian call for a universal poetry, with what I call "public surface" — a poetry with a very accessible commonsensual surface that can be understood by most everyone without a very literary education. But of course, if it was to rise above the level of journalism, it must have other subjective and/or subversive levels.

Well, I'm still on the same kick.

Most poets today still exist in a kind of poetry ghetto. They get pittances for published poems, compared to prose writers, even in mass media periodicals, if they manage to get in at all. And poetry readings don't begin to pay the rent for most.

What to do about it? How to get out of the poetry ghetto? The answer is obvious. Write poems that say something supremely original and supremely important, which everyone aches to hear, poetry that cries out to be heard, poetry that's news. And is it naive to think that even the mass media might print it or air it, if it were a new kind of news? Perhaps the poets would still be ignored by our dominant culture, because they're saying just what our materialist, technophiliac world doesn't want to hear. And the messenger with the unwelcome message will continue to be killed?

I would like to propose a regular monthly column in a daily newspaper with the title "Poetry As News." It would begin with great poems of the past that still are news. I think right off of Matthew Arnold's "Dover Beach":

Ah love let us be true
to one another!
For we are here as on a darkling plain
Swept with confused alarms of struggle and flight
Where ignorant armies clash by night . . .

I think also of course of Whitman's "I Hear America Singing," of poems by Homer, Shakespeare, W.B. Yeats, Cavafy, Pablo

Neruda, Marianne Moore, e.e.cummings, Kenneth Patchen, Kenneth Rexroth, Allen Ginsberg, and Adrienne Rich. I think of Bob Dylan's early songs and of the Beatles' "Yellow Submarine," of "The Great Paramita Sutra," and perhaps of the latest rap poetry at the Newyorican Café on the Lower East Side. And I think of the French poet Jacques Prévert whom I translated when I was a student in France:

THE DISCOURSE ON PEACE

Near the end of an extremely important discourse
the great man of state stumbling
on a beautiful hollow phrase
falls over it
and undone with gaping mouth
shows his teeth
gasping
and the dental decay of his peaceful reasoning
exposes the nerve of war
the delicate question of money

QUARTIER LIBRE

I put my cap in the cage
and went out with the bird on my head
So
one no longer salutes
asked the commanding officer
No
one no longer salutes
replied the bird
Ah good
excuse me I thought one saluted
said the commanding officer
You are fully excused everybody makes mistakes
said the bird

Above and beyond all this, poetic intuition and the intuitions
of great poetry still remain our best medium for fathoming
man's fate. In this vein, here are some proposed subjects for
poets to ponder:

Why is it dark at night, why is there darkness at night?
Is every orgasm a little death, or a little birth?
Is death male or female or neither?
La vida es sueno? Is life literally a dream? And, if so, when
will we truly awake?

October 1998

THE POETIC
CITY THAT WAS

The painter, who thought he was Stephan Dedalus in James Joyce's *Portrait of the Artist as a Young Man* setting forth to articulate the uncreated conscience of his race, saw San Francisco for the first time from the deck of an Oakland ferry some fifty years ago.

He had come overland by coach train from New York, having left Barcelona just a few weeks before. He'd been in Spain for several years on the G.I. Bill, learning the language and attending art school. And someone there had told him that San Francisco was the most European city, the most Italian city, the most polyglot city, the most bohemian city in America, except for Greenwich Village. He had no inclination to return to the heartless stone canyons of Manhattan where the art establishment seemed as entrenched as in Europe with no footholds offered to the young and unknown. And anyway, being a red wine addict, he was attracted by the rumor of San Francisco as the center of the only real wineregion in the United States. "All those dagos," someone had told him, "They're not going anywhere where you can't grow wine." That was enough for him, and to hell with the rest of wineless America.

Fifty years ago the city seemed an ideal place for a poet and artist to live, especially one who considered himself a kind of expatriate. He was to learn much later how so many poets and artists in America increasingly saw themselves as expatriates in their own country, a country in which the "subjective," or the "inner self," was increasingly under attack in a ravenous consumer society. In fact, Henry Miller had prophesied it all in his *The Air Conditioned Nightmare*, written upon his shocked return to the U.S. after many years in France. "Another breed of men has taken over," quoth Henry, or words to that effect. Greed would be king, but that wasn't evident in 1950s San Francisco, as our anti-hero prepared to land on the Barbary Coast.

Approaching the Ferry Building, he stood on deck and saw a small shining white city, looking rather like Tunis seen from seaward, a Mediterranean city, with small white houses on hillsides, brilliant in January sunshine. Near the Ferry

Building there were some larger, mostly white buildings that he later learned to call "highrises" — not really qualifying as skyscrapers by New York standards. And their clean sharp shadows had the look of early morning, though it was already past noon. It seemed an early morning city, rising up the hills, the air itself flashing with sunlight — that special San Francisco January light, so different from the pearly light of Paris beloved by painters.

He was the first off the ferry, with no idea where to go, except up. The city rose up before him as he started up Market Street, his sea bag over his shoulder, paint box underarm, still wearing his Basque beret.

He walked and walked and walked that day, and got the impression that the natives had a kind of island mentality, considering themselves San Franciscans first, on an island which wasn't necessarily a part of the United States. He felt right at home from the first. It seemed as ideal as any city could be for an artist or writer, perhaps like Athens at the height of Greek culture, or Dublin at the time of the Irish Renaissance — a city small enough for human conviviality and large enough for intense creative ferment, with a metropolitan sensibility.

It took him some time to discover North Beach, the Italian and bohemian center of the city. But in a few days he found a big sunny flat for sixty-five dollars a month and a huge painting studio for twenty-nine dollars. There was no electricity above the ground floor, and he had a pot-bellied stove for heat. There was a whole new school of poets brewing, and there were pioneering artists around the School of Fine Arts who later became famous as San Francisco Figurative painters and abstract expressionists. It was the last frontier, and they were dancing on the edge of the world.

Fifty years later, he awoke one fine morning like Rip Van Winkle and found himself again with his sea bag on his shoulder, looking for anywhere he could live and work. The new owners of his old flat now wanted $2500 a month, and his studio was $3000 plus. Many of his friends were also evicted, for it seemed their buildings weren't owned by San Franciscans anymore but by faceless investors with venture capital. Corporate monoculture had wiped out any unique sense of place, turning the "island-city" into an artistic theme-park, without artists. And he was on the street.

CHALLENGES TO YOUNG POETS

Invent a new language anyone can understand.

Climb the Statue of Liberty.

Reach for the unattainable.

Kiss the mirror and write what you see and hear.

Dance with wolves and count the stars, including the unseen.

Be naïve, innocent, non-cynical, as if you had just landed on earth (as indeed you have, as indeed we all have), astonished by what you have fallen upon.

Write living newspapers. Be a reporter from outer space, filing dispatches to some supreme managing editor who believes in full disclosure and has a low tolerance level for hot air.

Write an endless poem about your life on earth or elsewhere.

Read between the lines of human discourse.

Avoid the provincial, go for the universal.

Think subjectively, write objectively.

Think long thoughts in short sentences.

Don't attend poetry workshops, but if you do, don't go to learn "how to" but to learn "what" (What's important to write about).

Don't bow down to critics who have not themselves written great masterpieces.

Resist much, obey less.

Secretly liberate any being you see in a cage.

Write short poems in the voice of birds.
Make your lyrics truly lyrical. Birdsong is not
made by machines. Give your poem wings to
fly to the treetops.

The much-quoted dictum from William Carlos
Williams, "No ideas but in things," is OK for
prose, but it lays a dead hand on lyricism,
since "things" are dead.

Don't contemplate your navel in poetry and
think the rest of the world is going to think
it's important.

Remember everything, forget nothing.

Work on a frontier, if you can find one.

Go to sea, or work near water, and paddle
your own boat.

Associate with thinking poets. They're hard to find.

Cultivate dissidence and critical thinking. "First thought, best thought" may not make for the greatest poetry. First thought may be worst thought.

What's on your mind? What do you have in mind? Open your mouth and stop mumbling.

Don't be so open-minded that your brains fall out.

Question everything and everyone. Be subversive, constantly questioning reality and the status quo.

Be a poet, not a huckster. Don't cater, don't pander, especially not to possible audiences, readers, editors, or publishers.

Come out of your closet. It's dark in there.

Raise the blinds, throw open your shuttered
windows, raise the roof, unscrew the locks
from the doors, but don't throw away the
screws.

Be committed to something outside yourself.
Be militant about it. Or ecstatic.

To be a poet at sixteen is to be sixteen, to be
a poet at 40 is to be a poet. Be both.

Wake up and pee, the world's on fire.

Have a nice day.

*First read at the Seventeenth Annual San
Francisco High School Poetry Festival,
February 3, 2001.*

A NORTH BEACH SCENE

Away above a harborful
                    of caulkless houses
among the charley noble chimneypots
                of a rooftop rigged with clotheslines
    a woman pastes up sails
                        upon the wind
hanging out her morning sheets
                            with wooden pins
                O lovely mammal
                            her nearly naked breasts
            throw taut shadows
                        as she stretches up
to hang at last the last of her
                        so white washed sins
        but it is wetly amorous
                        and winds itself about her
            clinging to her skin
                        So caught with arms upraised
        she tosses back her head
                        in voiceless laughter
    and in choiceless gesture then

shakes out gold hair

while in the reachless seascape spaces

between the blown white shrouds

stand out the bright steamers

to kingdom come

THEY WERE PUTTING UP
THE STATUE . . .

They were putting up the statue
          of Saint Francis
    in front of the church
       of Saint Francis
                in the city of San Francisco
    in a little side street
                    just off the Avenue
    and the sun was coming up on time
                                in its usual fashion
      and just beginning to shine
                    on the statue of Saint Francis
        where no birds sang

And a lot of old Italians
                    were standing all around
    in the little side street
                    just off the Avenue
    watching the wily workers
                    who were hoisting up the statue

with a chain and a crane
                        and other implements
    And a lot of young reporters
                            in button-down clothes
        were taking down the words
                            of one young priest
        who was propping up the statue
                            with all his arguments
        And all the while
                while no birds sang
                        any Saint Francis Passion
and while the lookers kept looking
                        up at Saint Francis
        with his arms outstretched
                    to the birds which weren't there
a very tall and very purely naked
                                young virgin
    with very long and very straight
                        straw hair
        and wearing only a very small
                        bird's nest
        in a very existential place
                    kept passing thru the crowd

                                    all the while
                    and up and down the stairs
                                        in front of Saint Francis
her eyes downcast all the while
                            and singing to herself

D O G

The dog trots freely in the street
and sees reality
and the things he sees
are bigger than himself
and the things he sees
are his reality
Drunks in doorways
Moons on trees
The dog trots freely thru the street
and the things he sees
are smaller than himself
Fish on newsprint
Ants in holes
Chickens in Chinatown windows
their heads a block away
The dog trots freely in the street
and the things he smells
smell something like himself
The dog trots freely in the street
past puddles and babies
cats and cigars

poolrooms and policemen
He doesn't hate cops
He merely has no use for them
and he goes past them
and past the dead cows hung up whole
in front of the San Francisco Meat Market
He would rather eat a tender cow
than a tough policeman
though either might do
And he goes past the Romeo Ravioli Factory
and past Coit's Tower
and past Congressman Doyle of the Unamerican Committee
He's afraid of Coit's Tower
but he's not afraid of Congressman Doyle
although what he hears is very discouraging
very depressing
very absurd
to a sad young dog like himself
to a serious dog like himself
But he has his own free world to live in
His own fleas to eat
He will not be muzzled
Congressman Doyle is just another
fire hydrant

to him
The dog trots freely in the street
and has his own dog's life to live
and to think about
and to reflect upon
touching and tasting and testing everything
investigating everything
without benefit of perjury
a real realist
with a real tale to tell
and a real tail to tell it with
a real live
          barking
                democratic dog
engaged in real
               free enterprise
with something to say
                about ontology
something to say
               about reality
                         and how to see it
                                   and how to hear it
with his head cocked sideways
                    at streetcorners

as if he is just about to have
             his picture taken
                          for Victor Records
             listening for
                          His Master's Voice
          and looking
                   like a living questionmark
                                into the
                             great gramophone
                             of puzzling existence
     with its wondrous hollow horn
          which always seems
just about to spout forth

               some Victorious answer

               to everything

BASEBALL CANTO

Watching baseball
sitting in the sun
eating popcorn
reading Ezra Pound
and wishing Juan Marichal
would hit a hole right through
the Anglo-Saxon tradition
in the First Canto
and demolish the barbarian invaders
When the San Francisco Giants take the field
and everybody stands up to the National Anthem
with some Irish tenor's voice
piped over the loudspeakers
with all the players struck dead in their places
and the white umpires like Irish cops
in their black suits and little black caps
pressed over their hearts
standing straight and still
like at some funeral of a blarney bartender
and all facing East
as if expecting some Great White Hope

or the Founding Fathers
to appear on the horizon
like 1066 or 1776 or all that
But Willie Mays appears instead
in the bottom of the first
and a roar goes up
       as he clouts the first one into the sun
          and takes off
            like a footrunner from Thebes
     The ball is lost in the sun
         and maidens wail after him
          but he keeps running
            through the Anglo-Saxon epic
And Tito Fuentes comes up
    looking like a bullfighter
       in his tight pants and small pointed shoes
And the rightfield bleachers go mad
    with chicanos & blacks & Brooklyn beerdrinkers
       "Sweet Tito! Sock it to heem, Sweet Tito!"
And Sweet Tito puts his foot in the bucket
     and smacks one that don't come back at all
     and flees around the bases
  like he's escaping from the United Fruit Company
  as the gringo dollar beats out the Pound

        and Sweet Tito beats it out
        like he's beating out usury
        not to mention fascism and anti-semitism
And Juan Marichal comes up
  and the chicano bleachers go loco again
    as Juan belts the first fast ball
           out of sight
               and rounds first and keeps going
        and rounds second and rounds third
                    and keeps going
                    and hits pay-dirt
        to the roars of the grungy populace
As some nut presses the backstage panic button
for the tape-recorded National Anthem again
to save the situation
but it don't stop nobody this time
in their revolution round the loaded white bases
in this last of the great Anglo-Saxon epics
in the Territorio Libre of baseball

THE OLD ITALIANS DYING

For years the old Italians have been dying
all over America
For years the old Italians in faded felt hats
have been sunning themselves and dying
You have seen them on the benches
in the park in Washington Square
the old Italians in their black high button shoes
the old men in their old felt fedoras
                          with stained hatbands
have been dying and dying
                    day by day
You have seen them
every day in Washington Square San Francisco
the slow bell
tolls in the morning
in the Church of Peter & Paul
in the marzipan church on the plaza
toward ten in the morning the slow bell tolls
in the towers of Peter & Paul
and the old men who are still alive
sit sunning themselves in a row

on the wood benches in the park
and watch the processions in and out
funerals in the morning
weddings in the afternoon
slow bell in the morning Fast bell at noon
In one door out the other
the old men sit there in their hats
and watch the coming & going
You have seen them
the ones who feed the pigeons
                cutting the stale bread
                    with their thumbs & penknives
the ones with old pocketwatches
the old ones with gnarled hands
                        and wild eyebrows
the ones with the baggy pants
                        with both belt & suspenders
the grappa drinkers with teeth like corn
the Piemontesi the Genovesi the Siciliani
                smelling of garlic & pepperoni
the ones who loved Mussolini
the old fascists
the ones who loved Garibaldi
the old anarchists reading *L'Umanita Nuova*

the ones who loved Sacco & Vanzetti
They are almost all gone now
They are sitting and waiting their turn
and sunning themselves in front of the church
over the doors of which is inscribed
a phrase which would seem to be unfinished
from Dante's *Paradiso*
about the glory of the One
                              who moves everything . . .
The old men are waiting
for it to be finished
for their glorious sentence on earth
                              to be finished
the slow bell tolls & tolls
the pigeons strut about
not even thinking of flying
the air too heavy with heavy tolling
The black hired hearses draw up
the black limousines with black windowshades
shielding the widows
the widows with the long black veils
who will outlive them all
You have seen them
madre di terra, madre di mare

The widows climb out of the limousines
The family mourners step out in stiff suits
The widows walk so slowly
up the steps of the cathedral
fishnet veils drawn down
leaning hard on darkcloth arms
Their faces do not fall apart
They are merely drawn apart
They are still the matriarchs
outliving everyone
the old dagos dying out
in Little Italys all over America
the old dead dagos
hauled out in the morning sun
that does not mourn for anyone
One by one Year by year
they are carried out
The bell
never stops tolling
The old Italians with lapstrake faces
are hauled out of the hearses
by the paid pallbearers
in mafioso mourning coats & dark glasses
The old dead men are hauled out

in their black coffins like small skiffs
They enter the true church
for the first time in many years
in these carved black boats
                    ready to be ferried over
The priests scurry about
                as if to cast off the lines
The other old men
                        still alive on the benches
watch it all with their hats on
You have seen them sitting there
waiting for the bocce ball to stop rolling
waiting for the bell
                    to stop tolling & tolling
for the slow bell
                    to be finished tolling
telling the unfinished *Paradiso* story
as seen in an unfinished phrase
                    on the face of a church
as seen in a fisherman's face
in a black boat without sails
making his final haul

THE GREAT
CHINESE DRAGON

The great Chinese dragon which is the greatest dragon in all
the world and which once upon a time was towed across
the Pacific by a crew of coolies rowing in an open boat—
was the first real live dragon ever actually to reach these
shores

And the great Chinese dragon passing thru the Golden Gate
spouting streams of water like a string of fireboats then
broke loose somewhere near China Camp gulped down a
hundred Chinese seamen and forthwith ate up all the
shrimp in San Francisco Bay

And the great Chinese dragon was therefore forever after
confined in a Chinatown basement and ever since allowed
out only for Chinese New Year's parades and other
Unamerican demonstrations paternally watched-over by
those benevolent men in blue who represent our more
advanced civilization which has reached such a high state
of democracy as to allow even a few barbarians to carry
on their quaint native customs in our midst

And thus the great Chinese dragon which is the greatest
    dragon in all the world now can only be seen creeping out
    of an Adler Alley cellar like a worm out of a hole some-
    time during the second week in February every year when
    it sorties out of hibernation in its Chinese storeroom
    pushed from behind by a band of fortythree Chinese elec-
    tricians and technicians who stuff its peristaltic accor-
    dion-body up thru a sidewalk delivery entrance
And first the swaying snout appears and then the eyes at
    ground level feeling along the curb and then the head
    itself casting about and swaying and heaving finally up to
    the corner of Grant Avenue itself where a huge paper sign
    proclaims the World's Largest Chinatown
And the great Chinese dragon's jaws wired permanently
    agape as if by a demented dentist to display the Cadmium
    teeth as the hungry head heaves out into Grant Avenue
    right under the sign and raising itself with a great snort
    of fire suddenly proclaims the official firecracker start of
    the Chinese New Year
And the lightbulb eyes lighting up and popping out on coiled
    wire springs and the body stretching and rocking further
    and further around the corner and down Grant Avenue
    like a caterpillar rollercoaster with the eyes sprung out
    and waving in the air like the blind feelers of some

mechanical preying mantis and the eyes blinking on and
off with Chinese red pupils and tiny bamboo-blind eyelids
going up and down

And still the tail of the dragon in the Adler Alley cellar
uncoiling and unwinding out into the street with the
fortythree Chinese technicians still stuffing the dragon
out the hole in the sidewalk and the head of the dragon
now three blocks away in the middle of the parade of
fancy floats presided over by Chinese virgins

And here comes the St. Mary's Chinese Girls' Drum Corps and
here come sixteen white men in pith helmets beating big
bass drums representing the Order of the Moose and here
comes a gang of happy car salesmen disguised as Islam
Shriners and here comes a chapter of the Order of
Improved Red Men and here comes a cordon of motorcycle
cops in crash helmets with radios going followed by a
small papier-mâché lion fed with Nekko wafers and run by
two guys left over from a Ten-Ten festival which in turn is
followed by the great Chinese dragon itself gooking over
balconies as it comes

And the great Chinese dragon has eaten a hundred humans
and their legs pop out of his underside and are his walk-
ing legs which are not mentioned in the official printed
program in which he is written up as the Great Golden

Dragon made in Hong Kong to the specifications of the
Chinese Chamber of Commerce and he represents the
force and mystery of life and his head sways in the sky
between the balconies as he comes followed by six
Chinese boy scouts wearing Keds and carrying strings of
batteries that light up the dragon like a nighttime
freeway
And he has lain all winter among a heap of collapsed paper
lanterns and green rubber lizards and ivory backscratchers
with the iron sidewalk doors closed over his head but he
has now sprung up with the first sign of Spring like the
force of life itself and his head sways in the sky and gooks
in green windows as he comes
And he is a monster with the head of a dog and the body of
a serpent risen yearly out of the sea to devour a virgin
thrown from a cliff to appease him and he is a young man
handsome and drunk ogling the girls and he has high
ideals and a hundred sport shoes and he says No to
Mother and he is a big red table the world will never tilt
and he has big eyes everywhere thru which he sees all
womankind milkwhite and dove-breasted and he will eat
their waterflowers for he is the cat with future feet
wearing Keds and he eats cake out of pastry windows and
is hungrier and more potent and more powerful and more

omnivorous than the papier-mâché lion run by two guys
and he is the great earthworm of lucky life filled with
flowing Chinese semen and he considers his own and our
existence in its most profound sense as he comes and he
has no Christian answer to the existential question even
as he sees the spiritual everywhere translucent in the
material world and he does not want to escape the
responsibility of being a dragon or the consequences of
his long horny tail still buried in the basement but the
blue citizens on their talking cycles think that he wants to
escape and at all costs he must not be allowed to escape
because the great Chinese dragon is the greatest poten-
tial dragon in all the world and if allowed to escape from
Chinatown might gallop away up their new freeway at the
Broadway entrance mistaking it for a Great Wall of China
or some other barbarian barrier and so go careening along
it chewing up stanchions and signposts and belching forth
some strange disintegrating medium which might melt
down the great concrete walls of America and they are
afraid of how far the great Chinese dragon might really go
starting from San Francisco and so they have secretly and
securely tied down the very end of his tail in its hole
   so that

     this great pulsing phallus of life at the very end of

its parade at the very end of Chinatown gives one wild
orgasm of a shudder and rolls over fainting in the bright
night street since even for a dragon every orgasm is a lit-
tle death

And then the great Chinese dragon starts silently shrinking
and shriveling up and drawing back and back and back to
its first cave and the soft silk skin wrinkles up and shrinks
and shrinks on its sprung bamboo bones and the handsome
dejected head hangs down like a defeated prizefighter's
and so is stuffed down again at last into its private place
and the cellar sidewalk doors press down again over the
great wilted head with one small hole of an eye blinking
still thru the gratings of the metal doors as the great
Chinese dragon gives one last convulsive earthquake shake
and rolls over dead-dog to wait another white year for
the final coming and the final sowing of his oats and
teeth

GREAT AMERICAN
WATERFRONT POEM

San Francisco land's end and ocean's beginning The land the
sea's edge also The river within us the sea about us The
place where the story ended the place where the story
began The first frontier the last frontier Beginning of end
and end of beginning End of land and land of beginning
Embarcadero Freeway to nowhere turned into part of
Vaillancourt's "Wrecked Freeway Fountain" What is the
water saying to the sea on San Francisco waterfront where I
spent most of my divorce from civilization in and out water-
front hangouts China Basin Mission Rock Resort Public Fishing
Pier Harbor Lunch Tony's Bayview Red's Java House Shanty
Gallery Bottom-of-the-Mark Eagle Café Longshoreman's Hall
the Waterfront dead No Work No Pay Golden Gate Pilot Boat
in fog Podesta Divers SS American Racer rusty Mystic Mariner
Motorship Goy Mount Vernon Victory Red Stack Tugs standing
out past the pier where I telephoned the lawyers saying I
was shipping out on the sailing ship Balclutha and wouldn't
be back until they tore down the Embarcadero Freeway
along with the rest of petroleum civilization and the

literary-industrial complex far from where I'm standing
opposite Alcatraz by the thousand fishing boats nested in
green thick water The sea a green god feeding Filipino fish-
ermen on the quays Hawaiians in baseball caps and peajack-
ets retired Chief Petty officers casting live bait Puerto
Ricans with pile-worms in tincans Old capital N Negroes with
catfish called something else here The top of Angel Island
showing through fog funneled through Golden Gate Monday
morning October sun the Harbor Cruise boat tilting with
tourists into a fogbank Gulls on the roofs of piers asleep in
sun The Last Mohican eating his lunch out of a pail and
catching his next lunch with the last of it The phone booth
where I telephoned It's All Over Count Me Out The fog lifting
the sun the sun burning through The bright steamers stand-
ing out in the end of the first poem I ever wrote in San
Francisco twenty years ago just married on a rooftop in
North Beach overlooking this place I've come to in this life
this waterfront of existence A great view and here comes
more life The Western Pacific Freight Ferry ploughing across
the horizon between two piers foghorn blowing as I ask a
passing elderly ship captain in plaid suit and Tyrolean hat for
the time and he takes out his pocket chronometer which says
a quarter of two and tells me in thick Norwegian accent
"Quarrter to Tvelve" he just off a plane from Chicago no

doubt going to catch his ship for the Far East after visiting his aged mother in Minnesota Foghorns still sounding at the Golden Gate An old freighter light-in-the-water on headings adjusting its compass a pilot flag up and the captain on a wing of the bridge coffeemug in hand greatcoat collar up The wind beginning to come up blowing the fog away from the phone booth the phone dial very clear All of Angel Island now visible through the fogbank A red hull appears standing-in loaded to the gunnels with oil An Arab on the bridge his turban flying Passing Alcatraz he buys it The Last of the Mohicans reels in his line On the end of it a string of beads once lost in a trade for Manhattan Island The Belt Line Railroad engine stands snorting on a spur next to the Eagle Café with a string of flats & boxcars I park on the tracks imbedded in asphalt and enter the Eagle Café a sign on the wall saying "Save the Eagle—Last of an Endangered Species" and I get beer just as old brakeman runs in and shouts "Blue Volkswagen bus!" I rush out and save my bus from the train I see a clock and run for the phone on the pier where the lawyer's supposed to call me back at noon There's a dude in the booth with his address book out and a lot of coins spread out on the ledge He's dialing ten numbers He's putting the coins in very slowly He starts talking slowly He's really enjoying himself The tide is running out The Balclutha

strains at its moorings The guy in the booth has a lot to say
and lotsa time to say it He's in his own civilized world
enclosed in the booth of civilization and I'm in mine outside
waiting for my lawyer to call back with the final word on my
divorce from civilization Will they let Man be free or won't
they Will they or won't they let him be a barbarian or a
wanderer if he wants to I look at my reflection in the glass
of the phone booth outside It's like a mirror of the world
with a wild me in it and the Bank of America towering over
behind me Will Eros or Civilization win And who's this weirdo
who is myself and where does he think he's going to sail
away to when there isn't any longer any Away Another huge
oiler stands in All the fucked-up diplomats of the world on
the bridge holding empty champagne glasses as in a Fellini
movie The guy in the booth hangs up and falls out I sit down
in the booth and drink my beer waiting for the phone to ring
The Balclutha's whistle blows The tide is at the ebb
The phone rings

TWO SCAVENGERS IN A TRUCK, TWO BEAUTIFUL PEOPLE IN A MERCEDES

At the stoplight waiting for the light
                      Nine AM downtown San Francisco
  a bright yellow garbage truck
            with two garbagemen in red plastic blazers
  standing on the back stoop
               one on each side hanging on
  and looking down into
                 an elegant open Mercedes
    with an elegant couple in it
The man
      in a hip three-piece linen suit
        with shoulder-length blond hair & sunglasses
The young blond woman so casually coifed
            with a short skirt and colored stockings
  on the way to his architect's office
And the two scavengers up since Four AM
                 grungy from their route
      on the way home

The older of the two with grey iron-hair
                                    and hunched back
          looking down like some
                                    gargoyle Quasimodo
And the younger of the two
                              also with sunglasses & longhair
        about the same age as the Mercedes driver
And both scavengers gazing down
                                    as from a great distance
              at the cool couple
      as if they were watching some odorless TV ad
                  in which everything is always possible
And the very red light for an instant
                    holding all four close together
      as if anything at all were possible
                                    between them
        across that small gulf
                          in the high seas
                                    of this democracy

IN GOLDEN GATE
PARK THAT DAY . . .

In Golden Gate Park that day
                a man and his wife were coming along
     thru the enormous meadow
                    which was the meadow of the world
He was wearing green suspenders
                    and carrying an old beat-up flute
                                in one hand
     while his wife had a bunch of grapes
                    which she kept handing out
                                individually
                        to various squirrels
                                as if each
                        were a little joke
     And then the two of them came on
                        thru the enormous meadow
     which was the meadow of the world
                        and then
          at a very still spot where the trees dreamed
             and seemed to have been waiting thru all time

                                        for them
              they sat down together on the grass
                            without looking at each other
          and ate oranges
                      without looking at each other
                                and put the peels
          in a basket which they seemed
                          to have brought for that purpose
          without looking at each other
And then
          he took his shirt and undershirt off
  but kept his hat on
                      sideways
                            and without saying anything
          fell asleep under it
                            And his wife just sat there looking
at the birds which flew about
  calling to each other
                  in the stilly air
      as if they were questioning existence
              or trying to recall something forgotten
But then finally
              she too lay down flat

and just lay there looking up
                                        at nothing
yet fingering the old flute
                            which nobody played
and finally looking over
                            at him
without any particular expression
                                except a certain awful look
of terrible depression

A REPORT ON A HAPPENING IN WASHINGTON SQUARE, SAN FRANCISCO

When the lovely bride and groom came out onto the grand
front steps of the Catholic church of Saint Peter & Paul at
4:32 in the afternoon a knot of natives was waiting at the
bottom of the steps including a bunch of bridesmaids and
family friends all of whom were holding onto the straight
strings of bright green balloons which were the exact same
green as the bridesmaids' dresses And the bride was holding
onto a pure white balloon which was naturally the same as
her wedding gown and the groom was holding a black balloon
that matched his black tail coat And the newlyweds proceed-
ed to knot the strings of their two balloons together and
then with a kind of whoop let them soar away while at the
same instant all the people holding green balloons let theirs
go with a little cheer And the beatific bride and her hand-
some groom laughed and waved as they descended toward
the others with never a look up at the balloons that were

zooming straight up into the blue sky and becoming smaller and smaller every instant while the newlyweds gaily climbed onto the waiting imitation San Francisco Cable Car upon which the bridesmaids were already perched and nobody casting even a glance at the flying balloons that now seemed to be heading South over downtown San Francisco with the black and white balloons keeping close together on their tether while the green balloons started spreading out all over And the groom and bride took their special seats at the front of the cable car which wasn't a real cable car at all since it had rubber wheels not attached to any cable which would have restricted its destiny And the happy couple were still waving and laughing and kissing each other and then ringing and ringing the cable car bell while the balloons that nobody looked at were now at least a couple of miles high in the distant sky that now seemed to be growing darker and darker with huge banks of cirrus clouds to the West toward which the tiny balloons now turned like a flock of birds winging seaward with two of them still close together while the others strung out further and further so that they began to look like lost sheep in an alpine landscape of towering white mountains While the cable car of a sudden started up with a great clanging of its bell as everyone cheered and waved without ever a look at the disappearing balloons of

their lives so far away now that they looked like very distant
mountain climbers scaling the walls of great glaciers in the
final working out of their separate fates except for the two
climbers still roped together As the cable car zoomed off
westward on Filbert Street and on toward Russian Hill over
which in farthest sky still could be seen the tiny black dots
of the climbers going higher and higher and disappearing into
their destinies in which even the two roped together would
in the normal course of life lose their breath and shrivel
away and fall to earth out of air

THE ARTIST

The party hoppers
                    wolfing down the wine and cheese
    without a glance at what might be
                                    considered art
At all those Thursday evening openings
                        in San Francisco galleries
And the critics and the crickets
                    and the singles out to score
And the docents of the donor classes
                sheathed in silk & Christian Dior
                            holding long-stemmed glasses
With the tide of tinkled voices rising
And the painter to one side apprising
                    the whole uprising
                            as if from a most distant shore
    And saying to himself Is *this*
                        what I am painting for?
No wonder then that he
                    adrift in this society
    doth drink too much
                    and roll upon the floor?

THE GREEN
STREET MORTUARY
MARCHING BAND

The Green Street Mortuary Marching Band
  marches right down Green Street
    and turns into Columbus Avenue
     where all the café sitters at
       the sidewalk café tables
        sit talking and laughing and
         looking right through it
 as if it happened every day in
  little old wooden North Beach San Francisco
  but at the same time feeling thrilled
   by the stirring sound of the gallant marching band
   as if it were celebrating life and
        never heard of death
And right behind it comes the open hearse
 with the closed casket and the
   big framed picture under glass propped up
   showing the patriarch who
       has just croaked

And now all seven members of
        the Green Street Mortuary Marching Band
            with the faded gold braid on their
                                    beat-up captains' hats
                    raise their bent axes and
                        start blowing all more or less
                                        together and
        out comes this Onward Christian Soldiers like
                you heard it once upon a time only
                    much slower with a dead beat
And now you see all the relatives behind the
                closed glass windows of the long black cars and
                        their faces are all shiny like they
                            been weeping with washcloths and
                            all super serious
                like as if the bottom has just dropped out of
                    their private markets and
        there's the widow all in weeds, and the sister with
the bent frame and the mad brother who never got through
school and Uncle Louie with the wig and there they all are
assembled together and facing each other maybe for the
first time in a long time but their masks and public faces are
all in place as they face outward behind the traveling corpse
up ahead and oompah oompah goes the band very slow with

the trombones and the tuba and the trumpets and the big
bass drum and the corpse hears nothing or everything and
it's a glorious autumn day in old North Beach if only he could
have lived to see it Only we wouldn't have had the band who
half an hour later can be seen straggling back silent along
the sidewalks looking like hungover brokendown Irish
bartenders dying for a drink or a Last Hurrah

BOUNCER'S BAR

Passed the Bouncer's Bar tonight
in its old leaning building
just off the Embarcadero
Lots of stiffs in there
still nursing their beers
and staring at the wall
It was that kind of place
long on atmosphere
and short on talk
Even the bartender kept silent
having long ago given up bar banter
There was no Happy Hour in here
even in the bad old days
Nothing relieved the gloom
on days like this
The swinging door
rarely swung
The bums crept in out of the sun
Only the jukebox once in a while
showed signs of life
now and then letting out late at night

an old broken moan
about a dude leaving his wife
and how she done him wrong for a song
While an old head in a corner
mumbles and sings along
And falls out into the night
with its pathless starry sky
And raises a fist
to those black heavens
And lets out a bloody cry

I SAW ONE OF THEM

I saw one of them sleeping
        huddled under cardboard
                by the Church of Saint Francis
I saw one of them
           rousted by the priest
I saw one of them squatting in bushes
I saw another staggering
        against the plateglass window
                of a firstclass restaurant
I saw one of them in a phone booth
                shaking it
I saw one with burlap feet
I saw one in a grocery store
          come out with a pint
I saw another come out
        with nothing
I saw another putting a rope
         through the loops of his pants
I saw one
     with a bird on his shoulder

I saw one of them singing
                on the steps of City Hall
                                in the so cool city of love
I saw one of them trying to give
                                a lady cop a hug
I saw another sleeping
                by the Brooklyn Bridge
I saw another standing
                by the Golden Gate
The view from there was great

AT THE GOLDEN GATE

At the Golden Gate
A single plover far at sea
wings across the horizon
A single rower almost out of sight
rows his skull into eternity
And I take a buddha crystal in my hand
And begin becoming pure light

THE CHANGING LIGHT

The changing light at San Francisco

       is none of your East Coast light

         none of your

             pearly light of Paris

The light of San Francisco

       is a sea light

         an island light

And the light of fog

       blanketing the hills

      drifting in at night

       through the Golden Gate

          to lie on the city at dawn

And then the halcyon late mornings

     after the fog burns off

     and the sun paints white houses

          with the sea of light of Greece

      with sharp clean shadows

      making the town look like

         it had just been painted

But the wind comes up at four o'clock

          sweeping the hills

And then the veil of light of early evening
And then another scrim
        when the new night fog

               floats in
And in that vale of light
          the city drifts

             anchorless upon the ocean

YACHTS IN SUN

The yachts the white yachts
      with their white sails in sunlight
                  catching the wind and
                              heeling over
All together racing now
                  for the white buoy
            to tack about
                  to come about beyond it
And then come running in
            before the spanking wind
                  white spinnakers billowing
                        off Fort Mason San Francisco
Where once drowned down
            an Alcatraz con escaping
                  whose bones today are sand
                              fifty fathoms down
                        still imprisoned now
                              in the glass of the sea
As the so skillful yachts
                  freely pass over

TO THE
ORACLE AT DELPHI

Great Oracle, why are you staring at me,
do I baffle you, do I make you despair?
I, Americus, the American,
wrought from the dark in my mother long ago,
from the dark of ancient Europa —
Why are you staring at me now
in the dusk of our civilization —
Why are you staring at me
as if I were America itself
the new Empire
vaster than any in ancient days
with its electronic highways
carrying its corporate monoculture
around the world
And English the Latin of our days —

Great Oracle, sleeping through the centuries,
Awaken now at last
And tell us how to save us from ourselves

and how to survive our own rulers
who would make a plutocracy of our democracy
in the Great Divide
between the rich and the poor
in whom Walt Whitman heard America singing

O long-silent Sybil,
you of the winged dreams,
Speak out from your temple of light
as the serious constellations
with Greek names
still stare down on us
as a lighthouse moves its megaphone
over the sea
Speak out and shine upon us
the sea-light of Greece
the diamond light of Greece

Far-seeing Sybil, forever hidden,
Come out of your cave at last
And speak to us in the poet's voice
the voice of the fourth person singular
the voice of the inscrutable future
the voice of the people mixed

with a wild soft laughter--
And give us new dreams to dream,
Give us new myths to live by!

*Read at Delphi, Greece, on March 21, 2001 at the UNESCO
World Poetry Day*

L to R: Shigeyoshi Murao (City Lights Bookstore Manager), Jake Ehrlich, one of
the defense attorneys, Lawrence Ferlinghetti in the courtroom at the trial of
Allen Ginsberg's HOWL and Other Poems published by City Lights (1956). The
charges of obscenity were defeated and the publishers exonerated.
City Lights Collection

Ferlinghetti on the TransSiberian Railway USSR (February 1967)
© Heiner Bastian

Ferlinghetti reading poetry at KQED, San Francisco (February 18, 1957)
City Lights Collection

L to R: Russian poet Andrei Voznesensky, Ferlinghetti, Berlin (February 1967)
© Heiner Bastian

City Lights Bookstore (1969)
© Hammond Guthrie

Ferlinghetti at City Lights (1956)
City Lights Collection

With William S. Burroughs signing his books at City Lights (1980)
© Ira Nowinski

L to R: Gregory Corso, Ferlinghetti in Puccini Café, North Beach, San
Francisco (May 1981)
© Chris Felver

ABOVE
L to R: Ferlinghetti, Allen Ginsberg at City Lights (1981)
© Katy Raddatz

RIGHT
Ferlinghetti at Jack Kerouac's grave, Lowell, Massachusetts (1978)
© Helen V. MacLeod

L to R: Jazz poet Ted Joans, Ferlinghetti, on Grant Avenue in North Beach, San
Francisco (1981)
© Ira Nowinski

L to R: Nancy J. Peters, Editor, City Lights Books, Ferlinghetti, at
City Lights (1980)
© Ira Nowinski

Ferlinghetti in his studio, Hunter's Point, San Francisco (1981)
© Joe Wolberg

Ferlinghetti in Tangier (1970s)
© Fabrizio Garghetti, ARCHIVIO FOTOGRAFICO

LAWRENCE FERLINGHETTI has lived in San Francisco since 1950. He is a bookman, painter, and author of many books, including the recently published How to Paint Sunlight (poetry) and Love in the Days of Rage (novel).

THE POET LAUREATE SERIES is made possible by support from San Francisco Grants for the Arts, the ArtsCouncil, the Zellerbach Fund, and the W.A. Gerbode Fund.

CITY LIGHTS FOUNDATION is a nonprofit foundation that supports literacy and the literary arts.

All contributions are gratefully accepted and fully tax deductible.